W9-BKV-674

DISCARD

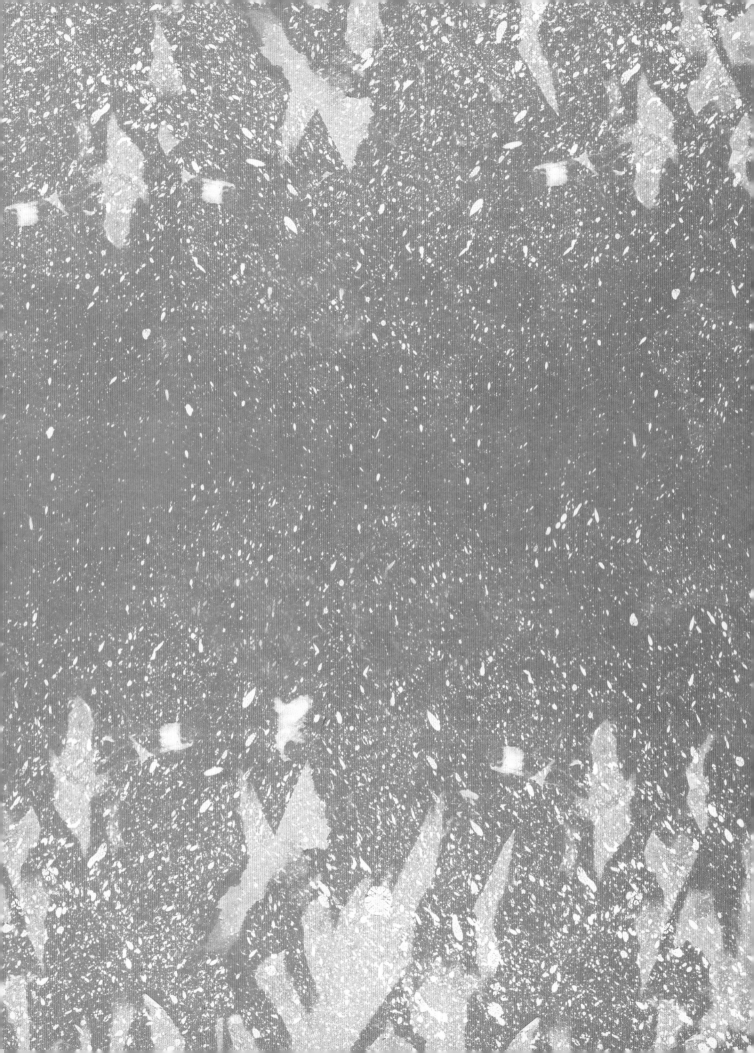

MARILYN SINGER & ED YOUNG

A STRANGE PLACE TO CALL HOME

THE WORLD'S MOST DANGEROUS HABITATS
& THE ANIMALS THAT CALL THEM HOME

chronicle books·san francisco

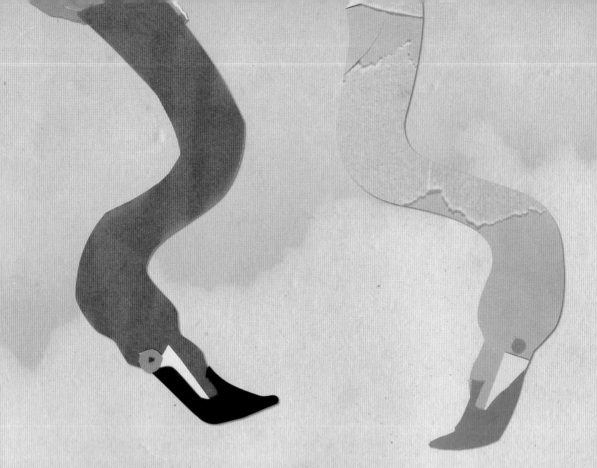

To Steve Coyle and Maryrose Hightower-Coyle —M. S.
To the lesson we may yet learn from the adaptabilities of the animal kingdom —E. Y.

Special thanks to:
Felicity Arengo (American Museum of Natural History), Steve Aronson, Brenda
Bowen, John Hare (www.wildcamels.com), Zack Lemann (Audubon Insectarium),
Mark Myers (Woodland Park Zoo), Kenneth Nickerson (School of Biological Sciences,
University of Nebraska–Lincoln), Louis Sorkin (American Museum of Natural
History), Paul Sweet (American Museum of Natural History), and to my wonderful
editor, Melissa Manlove, and the crew at Chronicle.

Text © 2012 by Marilyn Singer.
Illustrations © 2012 by Ed Young.
All rights reserved. No part of this book may be reproduced in any form without
written permission from the publisher.

Library of Congress Cataloging-in-Publication Data available.
ISBN 978-1-4521-0120-0

Design by Sara Gillingham.
Typeset in Populaire and Chronicle Text.
The illustrations in this book were rendered in collage.
Manufactured in China.

MIX
Paper from
responsible sources
FSC® C104723

10 9 8 7 6 5 4 3 2

Chronicle Books LLC
680 Second Street, San Francisco, California 94107

www.chroniclekids.com

R0440835978

RISKY PLACES

Where would you rather live—in a lush forest where there is a lot of food and water and where it's always warm, or in a barren desert where there's little water and the daytime temperature is often above 100 degrees F? Would you prefer a home on a tropical reef teeming with life or inside a glacier where it's freezing?

It's true that large numbers of diverse animal species inhabit rainforests and coral reefs, where the temperature is just right and there's plenty to eat and drink. However, because so many creatures live in these habitats, competition for food and space is fierce and refuge from predators can be tough to find.

Extreme environments such as deserts, glaciers, salt lakes, and pools of oil may not seem appealing, yet in these places, there is often less competition and more safety from predators. So over time, a variety of animals have adapted to these challenging conditions. This collection of poems celebrates some of these great adapters and the risky places where they live.

THINK COLD

Humboldt penguins

Hear "penguins," think cold,
    think riding on floes.
Who pictures them swimming
    where it seldomly snows,
on the dry, dry coasts
    of Chile and Peru,
with no ice to slide on,
    no glaciers to view?
Where they have to dig burrows
    with bills and with legs,
so the scorching sun
    won't hard-boil
    each precious clutch of eggs?
Which adaptation is the bolder:
    to live where it's arid,
    or where it's colder?

THINK HEAT

snow monkeys

Hear "monkeys," think heat, think swinging in trees.
Who imagines them huddled in minus degrees,
heads white with snow from the latest storm,
on their isolated island, trying to keep warm,
submerged in a hot spring, taking a bath?
How did they get there? What was their path?
Why did they stay? Did they feel they were trapped?
Who first got the message:
We have to adapt?

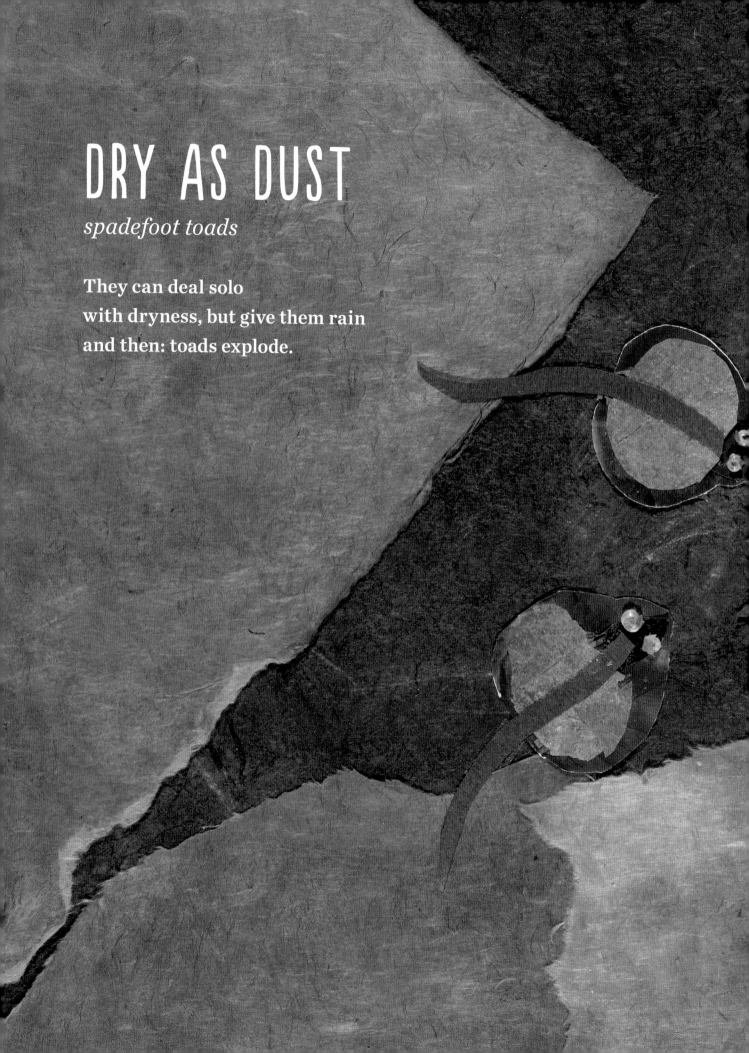

DRY AS DUST

spadefoot toads

They can deal solo
with dryness, but give them rain
and then: toads explode.

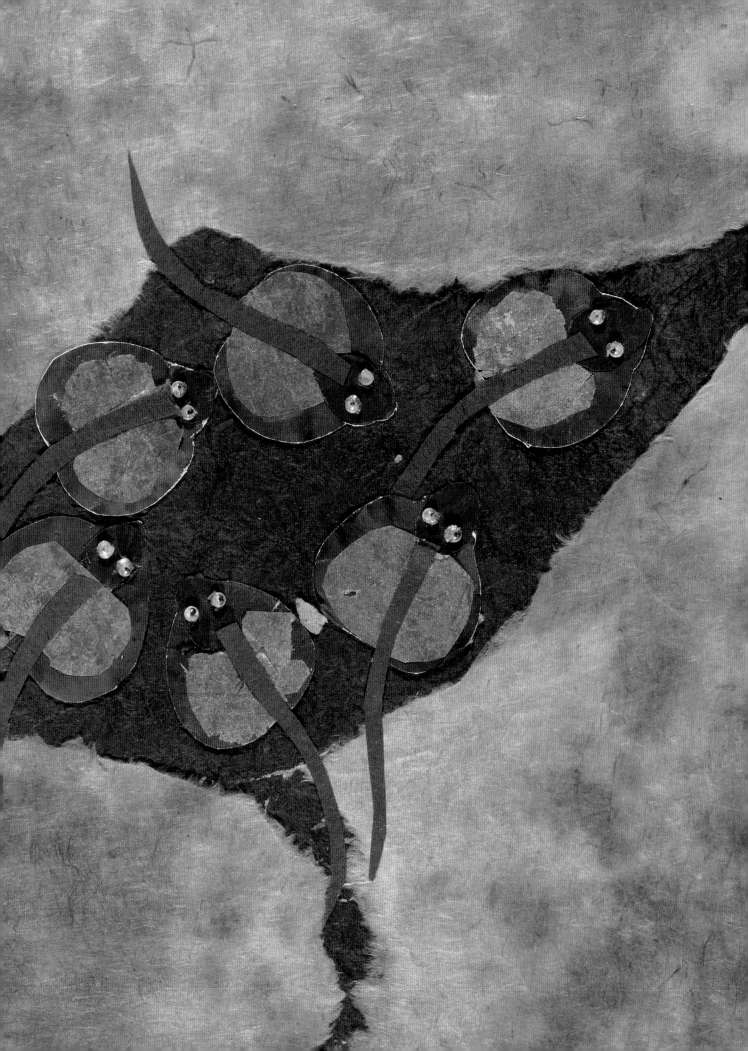

FROZEN SOLID

ice worms

If wriggling in the richest earth,
If hiding under leaves and logs . . .
If fastened to a coral reef,
If burrowed down in mucky bogs . . .

If writhing in a swimming pool,
Or in a collie's water dish,
Or in a sparrow's concrete bath . . .
If in the guts of cat or fish . . .

If buried in the mud or sand,
If lurking in the deepest seas,
Why not beneath the glacial ice,
     helped by their own antifreeze?

OUT OF SIGHT

blind cave fish

In these caves the blind are not bats,
      but fish.
Small, pink, eyeless,
they navigate their pools with confidence,
easily avoiding obstacles.
Crystals, cave pearls, fellow fish,
      no indecision, no collision.
Who needs vision
as long as this world remains
      so wet
      so dark?

SALT OF THE EARTH

flamingos

This harsh and salty land
(it's not a place to mock)—
Flamingos find it grand.

No palm trees or pink sand,
It's where they come to flock—
This harsh and salty land.

In saline lakes they stand,
No grassy lawn, no dock.
Flamingos find it grand

To feast at their command.
Here, brine shrimp are in stock.
This harsh and salty land

Demands a life well-planned
By each bird's daily clock.
Flamingos find it grand.

Here's to this hardy band!
It may come as a shock:
This harsh and salty land—
Flamingos find it grand.

DOWN IN THE DEPTHS

tube worms

Life is hard—it gets intense
       by deep-sea hydrothermal vents.
Superheated water rising,
       spouting out from tall, surprising
chimneys built on the ocean floor.
Yet there live giant worms galore
       in tubes that shield them from the heat.
They don't have mouths. They cannot eat.
Bacteria that live inside
       these creatures keep them well supplied
         with necessary nutrients.
Odd partnerships make lots of sense
       around these hydrothermal vents.

TOP OF THE WORLD

mountain goats

Atop a rocky peak, the air is pure,
  but the wind blows fierce and the climb is steep.
Each step must be confident and so sure,
  there's little need to look before you leap.
The ice, the snow, the winter's biting cold
  require a cozy, insulated coat.
What animal lives here, hardy and bold?
  Behold this king of cliffs, the mountain goat!
Feasting in springtime on grass that is lush,
  avoiding in summer the sun's blazing rays.
Browsing in autumn on stubborn dry brush,
  learning to deal with the year's hardest days.
Living where enemies cannot intrude,
  it succeeds indeed at this altitude.

ON THE ROCKS

limpets

In the intertidal zone,
        where waves are prone
to be forceful,
        where the waters rush
to batter, buffet, crush,
        dislodge, displace, fling,
a limpet is resourceful.
        Its fine construction
employs suction.
        In other words, its thing
is mightily to cling.

WALL OF SAND

camels

They know that swirl, that humming
On this quiet afternoon.
They can feel a storm is coming

Carried here by this simoon—
The wind that darkens sun and sky,
That moves the highest dune.

But see, these camels can defy
This sweeping wall of sand
If they need to, they will lie.

If possible, they'll stand
Till it's clear the peril's passed.
They are built well for this land.

They know just how to outlast.

A FISH IN THE AIR

mudskippers

Welcome to this mangrove stand.
Go on, you're allowed to stare.
Here, fishes walk on mud and sand.
Welcome to this mangrove stand,
Not quite water, not quite land.
Here, fishes perch to breathe the air.
Welcome to this mangrove stand.
Go on, you're allowed to stare.

A BIRD IN THE WATER

dippers

Gray as wet slate,
  bathtub-toy small,
the dipper dares
  the waterfall
to snatch a mayfly.
  to rest,
to nest uncertain
  in a rocky nook
two inches tall
  behind the rushing curtain.
Sure of feet and sure of wings
  a bird that weathers spray and foam,
the dipper sings
  where little else can live
and calls a tall cascade
  its home.

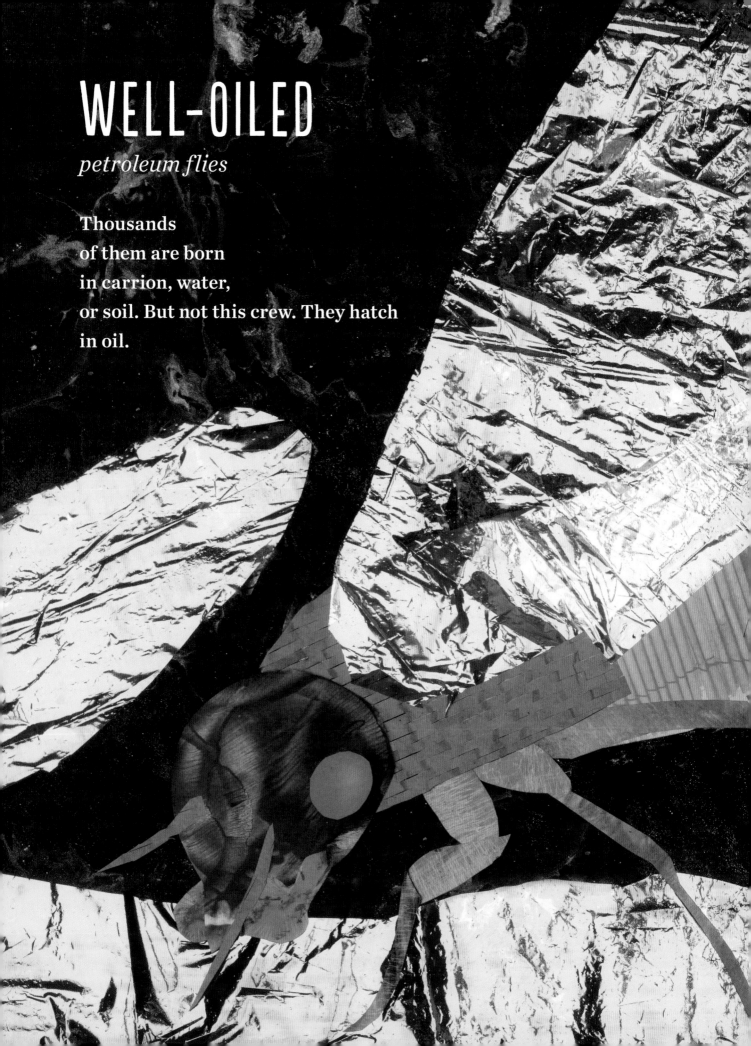

WELL-OILED

petroleum flies

Thousands
of them are born
in carrion, water,
or soil. But not this crew. They hatch
in oil.

CITY LIVING

urban foxes

They have
quit forests and
fields for sheds, flowerbeds;
forfeited wild berries for shrimp
lo mein.

It seems
an easy life,
but in close quarters, cars,
capture, and contagion take
their toll.

Foxes
adapted to
city living find it
full of plenty—but plentiful
in risk.

ENDNOTES

HUMBOLDT PENGUINS

Known as "warm weather" penguins (though the water is still quite cold on the coasts of Chile and Peru), Humboldt penguins (*Spheniscus humboldti*), unlike Antarctic species, don't have to hold eggs on their feet or build nests of stones. Instead, they dig burrows to avoid the sun and lay their eggs inside. Like other penguins, they are sociable, so the burrows are close together. This arrangement gives them protections from predatory birds such as gulls and skuas, but it hasn't protected them from humans who have hunted them for their meat or disturbed their colonies for guano (feces) to use as fertilizer.

SNOW MONKEYS

Snow monkeys (*Macaca fuscata*) do indeed live in troops varying in size from ten to several hundred or even larger on main and outlying Japanese islands, where the temperature drops as low as 5 degrees Fahrenheit (-15 degrees Celsius). They are the only monkeys to live that far north of the equator. Though during the winter nights they sleep in trees or huddled together on the ground, they are famous for their daytime bathing in hot springs to stay warm. Though they are a popular tourist attraction, many macaques are killed by farmers whose crops they raid. In addition, some troops have suffered losses because of habitat destruction.

SPADEFOOT TOADS

Spadefoot toads (*Spea* spp. and others) are found in arid areas all over the United States. These amphibians spend much of their life buried underground, dormant. But when it rains, they awake, come to the surface to eat and to find any puddle or pool in which to mate, and lay eggs. Then they dig burrows with their spade-shaped feet and go underground again. Among several species, their eggs can hatch within a day and turn from tadpoles to adults in one to two weeks, before the water dries up. Like their parents, the new toads will also burrow and remain dormant underground until it rains again.

ICE WORMS

There are many, many species of worms, and they are found everywhere—from earthworms beneath the soil to feather duster worms on tropical reefs; from knots of long, thin Gordian worms that can turn up in a toilet bowl or a dog's water dish to tapeworms that might live inside your pet. Ice worms (*Mesenchytraeus solifugus*) sound like a myth, but they're real. These half-inch-long relatives of earthworms live by the billions deep inside the glaciers and ice fields of northwestern America and Canada. In warmer weather, they come up to the surface to feed on algae, pollen, and other microscopic food. In the winter, they burrow into the ice and lie dormant. Their bodies have cell membranes and enzymes that are resistant to such cold temperatures. Scientists are studying their "antifreeze" for clues to ways life might exist on cold moons and planets and to ways of keeping organs cold for transplants. Some even hope the worms will help in the development of *cryonics*—the method of freezing people or animals who have just died of a severe illness—in hopes that they may be revived and healed in the future when a cure is found for their disease.

BLIND CAVE FISH

Fish in caves? Yes. Blind cave fish (*Astyanax mexicanus*) are freshwater fish that live in deep underground caves in Texas and Mexico. They have no eyes and they are *albino*—their skin is pink-white, with no pigmentation. Why? Because in the darkness, they don't need to see and they don't need pigmentation to protect them from sunburn. How do they navigate? By means of their *lateral line*—a sense organ that runs along each side of their bodies from their gills to their tail. This organ detects changes in water pressure and helps the fish to avoid obstacles and predators and also to find food.

P.S. The phrase "blind as a bat" is a popular saying because of the way bats use sonar to navigate. They are, however, not blind!

FLAMINGOS

We picture flamingos (*Phoenicopterus* spp.) in lush, tropical environments. But these birds actually live in a variety of habitats—some of them quite harsh, such as salt flats (barren plains encrusted with salt). How can these birds thrive in such places? For one thing, few predators live there. For another, the saline lakes in these areas are loaded with the flamingos' favorite foods: brine shrimp and other small invertebrates. Flamingos use their large bills to take in this fare along with mud and salt water. Their thick tongues pump out the liquids. Strainers in their beaks trap the food, which the flamingos then swallow. The birds can also excrete excess salt from glands in their noses. Their scaly legs are resistant to salt and chemical damage. They will drink and bathe in freshwater from springs or puddles when it is available, but they can survive without it.

TUBE WORMS

Some parts of the earth's seabed are slowly moving apart. As they move, cracks form. Seawater seeps into these cracks and is heated by *magma*—molten rock deep in the earth—to temperatures far above boiling. The water spews back out like a geyser, carrying with it many minerals. When this superheated water reaches the cold ocean water, the minerals clump and form amazing chimney-like shapes. It would seem that few animals could live around these hot vents, but tube worms (*Riftia pachyptila*) are among the creatures that can. These giants, which can grow to nearly eight feet long, have a *symbiotic*—mutually beneficial—partnership with bacteria that live inside them. The bacteria can convert chemicals in the water to supply the worms with nutrients, and the worms supply the bacteria with shelter and hydrogen sulfide for their own nutrition.

MOUNTAIN GOATS

Mountaintops are exposed to the elements—there is little shelter from wind, rain, sun, or cold. Few animals are able to live at such heights. One of those that does is the mountain goat (*Oreamnos americanus*), a creature that can leap twelve feet in a single bound. In the winter it is protected from the fierce weather by its woolly double-layered coat. In the spring, it sheds the outer layer. Mountain goats are *herbivores*—they eat grass and other plants, and they also get nutrients from mineral or salt licks. They must spend much of their time traveling in search of food, as well as shelter. Their specialized cloven hooves, with rough inner pads that grip and toes that can be spread apart for balance, allow the foraging goats to be sure-footed on these steep cliffs.

LIMPETS

The intertidal zone is the area along coastlines where the tides rise and fall. It is an extreme habitat—pounded by waves when the tides rush in and exposed to heat and sunlight when the water is low. Along rocky shores, a large group of small mollusks—animals that usually have shells—called limpets (*Patellogastropoda* and others) are among the creatures that meet these challenges. Each limpet has a muscular foot moistened with mucus. The foot allows the limpet to slide around, looking for algae to eat, and it also works like a suction cup to hold on to the rock surface. It is very difficult to pull a limpet off its rock. To avoid drying out during low tide, a limpet traps some water in its shell—enough to last until the waves rush in once more.

CAMELS

The camel (*Camelus* spp.) is able to live in deserts and other dry regions where other mammals could not easily survive. These "ships of the desert," long used by people for transportation, can eat plants that most other animals cannot digest. Their humps (the dromedary camel has one hump; the Bactrian has two) are used to store fat as an extra food supply, not water. Camels can go for a week or more without water, and then drink up to thirty-two gallons at one time, retaining the water in their blood cells without any ill effects. To deal with wind-blown sand, camels can shut their nostrils. Their eyes are protected by two rows of thick lashes and a clear inner eyelid that closes, but still allows the animal to see. During a sandstorm, a camel will keep walking on its large, broad feet unless the storm is too fierce. Then (sometimes urged by its handler), it will lie down to wait out the storm.

MUDSKIPPERS

Found only in tropical and subtropical areas where *mangroves*—a variety of trees and shrubs that grow in salty water—are found, mudskippers (*Periophthalmus* spp. and others) are truly strange fish. Their large eyes sit on top of their heads so they can look around while they stay underwater. But they can also move on land, using their bendable fins to walk and to climb up roots and rocks. They can even "skip," flipping themselves over mud and water. Like other fish, in the water mudskippers breathe through their gills. But on land they breathe air through their moist skin and through the lining of their mouth and throat.

DIPPERS

Most songbirds spend their lives in trees, but not the dipper (*Cinclus spp.*). It is the only songbird that can dive, swim, and feed underwater. It paddles with its feet and uses its wings to stay submerged. Its feathers are waterproofed by oil from a large *preen gland*. Found near clear streams and by waterfalls, the dipper eats aquatic insects and occasionally fish and fish eggs. It gets its name from the way it bobs its head for food, dipping as often as sixty times per minute.

PETROLEUM FLIES

Different types of flies are found all over the world and in every kind of climate. Some live in habitats that would kill most other beings. Among those are petroleum or oil flies (*Helaeomyia petrolei*). The larvae hatch in naturally occurring pools of oil, feeding on insects trapped in the petroleum. Then they pupate—transform into adults—on nearby grass. The adults live in cracks in the soil near the pools. They can walk on the oil as long as only their feet touch the surface.

URBAN FOXES

In the past hundred years, cities and suburbs have expanded and woodlands have shrunk. Red foxes (*Vulpes vulpes*) are forest animals, but they are remarkably adaptable and have moved into human settlements, where they use sheds, garages, flowerbeds, and other places for their dens. Omnivorous, they find plenty to eat in garbage pails and dumps, as well as fruit and vegetable gardens. But the cities are fraught with dangers, too. Urban foxes are killed by automobiles and diseases. They are also captured and removed. Some city dwellers think of them as pests, but others are excited to see these wild animals in our midst. In either case, their story tells how much we humans have changed the landscape and the lives of many animals on this planet.

ABOUT POETRY FORMS

Some poems don't rhyme or rhyme irregularly, and they have no strict form. They're called *free verse*. In this book, "A Bird in the Water" and "Out of Sight" are examples of free verse. Other poems have regular rhyme schemes, but no set rules. If we give the last word of each line a letter and say that *a* rhymes with *a*, *b* with *b*, etc., can you figure out the rhyme schemes for these poems: "Think Cold," "Think Heat," "Down in the Depths," "Frozen Solid," and "On the Rocks"?

Then there are poems written in such strict forms that we have given them names. Here is the list of poems in this book written in these forms:

"A Fish in the Air": *triolet*

"Dry as Dust": *haiku*

"Top of the World": *sonnet*

"Well-Oiled" and "City Living": *cinquain*

"Salt of the Earth": *villanelle*

"Wall of Sand": *terza rima*

And here is a website that explains all of these forms and more: www.poetryfoundation.org/learning/glossary-terms?category=forms-and-types.

Once you know about different types of poems, you can pick your favorite—free verse, informal rhyme, or a set form—and write your own poem about an animal with a strange home or one in your own backyard or, well, anything at all!

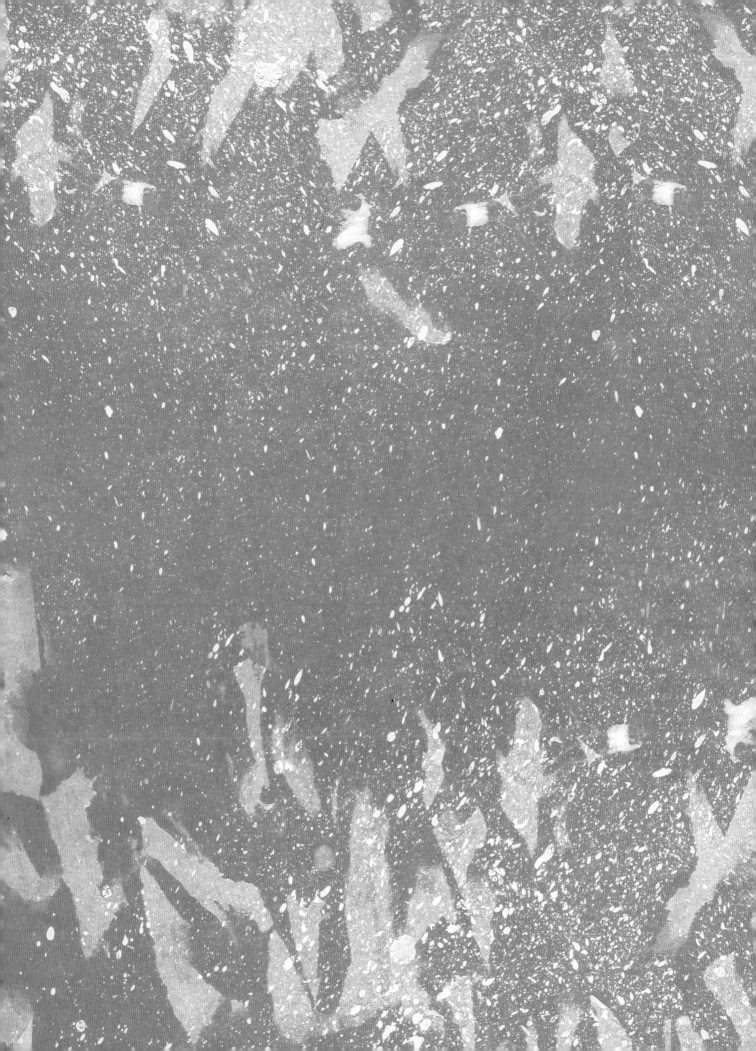